Washington

Washington

WILLIAM JAY JACOBS

CHARLES SCRIBNER'S SONS • NEW YORK
Collier Macmillan Canada • Toronto
Maxwell Macmillan International Publishing Group
New York • Oxford • Singapore • Sydney

Copyright © 1991 by William Jay Jacobs

Charles Scribner's Sons Books for Young Readers
Macmillan Publishing Company · 866 Third Avenue, New York, NY 10022
Collier Macmillan Canada, Inc.
1200 Eglinton Avenue East, Suite 200 · Don Mills, Ontario M3C 3N1

First Edition   10 9 8 7 6 5 4 3 2 1
Printed in the United States of America

Library of Congress Cataloging-in-Publication Data
Jacobs, William Jay.
Washington / William Jay Jacobs. — 1st ed.   p.   cm.
Summary: A biography of the first president of the United States describing his
youth in Virginia, his military career, his role in the formation of an independent
nation, and his leadership of that nation.
1. Washington, George, 1732–1799—Juvenile literature.
2. Presidents—United States—Biography—Juvenile literature.
3. Generals—United States—Biography—Juvenile literature.
4. United States.   Continental Army—Biography—Juvenile literature.
[1. Washington, George, 1732–1799.   2. Presidents.]   I. Title.
E312.66.J33 1991   973.4'1'092—dc20
[B]   [92]   90–8844 CIP AC ISBN 0-684-19275-6

Frontispiece portrait by John Vanderlyn. Office of the Architect of the Capitol.
Photograph on page 40 courtesy Mount Vernon Ladies' Association.
Photo research by Photosearch, Inc., New York

*For Manny and Leo, heirs to our nation's past,
shapers of its future . . .*

George Washington (on dais, at right) at the Constitutional Convention. Painting by Thomas Rossiter. *Independence National Historical Park.*

*A*ll of us think we know about George Washington. Of course. He was the first president of the United States. He was the little boy who, after chopping down a cherry tree, is supposed to have said, "I cannot tell a lie. I did it, Father." In paintings he often is shown riding a snow-white horse or gazing off into the distance. His face peers out at us from the dollar bill: stern, unsmiling, old, distant.

The real George Washington was a very different person—and a much more interesting one. Though hungry for fame and power, he also longed to be left alone to farm his land. A man of great charm and gentleness, he had a temper so violent that it took all of his iron will to control it. Adored and cheered as a great hero, he often felt unsure of his ability. He feared that he would fail and that people would blame him. Yet, through most of his adult life, Washington knew that the very survival of America—the country that he loved—depended on him.

George was born on February 22, 1732, on a large farm, or plantation, in Virginia, but one not nearly so large as those of Virginia's wealthiest families—the Byrds, the Carters, and the Randolphs. His father, Augustine Washington, had been married once before. George was the first child of his father's second marriage. When Augustine Washington's first wife died, there were three children to be cared for. He chose as his new bride Mary Ball, a woman in her early twenties, nearly fourteen years younger than he was. Within seven years after George's birth the couple had five more children.

Then, in 1743, when George was only eleven years old, his father suddenly became ill and died. His mother had to bring up George by herself. Barely able to read and write, she always feared that she and the children would lose their land and become poor. She also was afraid they might be hurt. So she tried to protect them. She tried to keep George close to the farmhouse instead of letting him roam, as he wanted to do. She would not let him ride his pony to school alone, like the other boys, but had a servant ride ahead of him.

George did not argue with his mother. He just remained silent. Perhaps to prove himself to his friends he looked for more and more dangerous ways to play—

A Currier & Ives print of Washington's birthplace at Bridges Creek, Westmoreland County, Virginia. *Museum of the City of New York.*

like breaking in wild horses. Soon he became known as a boy who was afraid of nothing.

When George's father died, he left most of his property to Lawrence and Augustine, the two sons of his first marriage. Both boys traveled in Europe and were educated at fine schools in England.

George had to make do with whatever formal education he could get in backwoods Virginia. In those days, that was not much. He learned geography and mathematics (which he liked) and read some English literature and the Bible.

Rules of Civility & Decent Behaviour
In Company and Conversation

1 Every Action done in Company, ought to ___ with Some Sign of Respect, to those that are present.

2 When in Company, put not your Hands to any Part of the Body, not usualy Discovered.

3 Shew to ___ thing to your friend that may affright him.

4 In the presence of Others Sing not to yourself with a humming ___ nor Drum with your Fingers or Feet.

5 If you Cough, Sneeze, Sigh, or Yawn, do it not Loud but privately; and Speak not in your Yawning, but put your hand before ___ face & turn aside.

6 Sleep not when others Speak, Sit not when others stand, Speak not when you Should hold your Peace, walk not on when others Stop.

7 Put not off your Cloths in the presence of Others, nor go out ___ Chamber half Drest.

8 At Play and at Fire its Good manners to Give Place to the last Commer, and affect not to Speak Louder than Ordinary.

9 Spit not in the Fire, nor Stoop low before it neither Put your Hands into the Flames to warm them, nor Set your Feet upon the Fire specially if there be meat before it.

10 When you Sit down, Keep your Feet firm and Even, without putting one on the other or Crossing them.

11 Shift not yourself in the Sight of others nor Gnaw your nails.

12 Shake not the head, Feet, or Legs row not the Eys lift not ___ one eyebrow higher than the other wry not the mouth, and bedew no man's face with your Spittle, by approaching ___ when you Speak.

At the age of thirteen he copied into his notebook 110 "Rules of Civility and Decent Behavior"—advice for boys on how to be polite and cultured adults. Young people were told, for example: "Sleep not when others Speak"; "Sit not when others stand"; "Speak not when you should hold your Peace. . . ."; "In the Presence of Others sing not to yourself with a humming Noise, nor Drum with your fingers or feet. . . ."

Young George Washington probably had no more than seven or eight years of formal schooling. Unlike his half brothers, Lawrence and Augustine, he never went to college. But at Lawrence's handsome estate, Mount Vernon, on the Potomac, he learned other lessons. He learned to shoot and to ride. He learned the gracious manners of a Virginia gentleman. He learned to dance and to play cards and billiards. He learned to control his temper. And he learned that a gentleman must be ready to give up his own ease and comfort for the good of the community.

By the time George was sixteen, he also began to enjoy the company of girls. He came to like one of them, Sally Cary, especially well. But when Sally was eighteen she married a son of Colonel William Fairfax and went to live at Belvoir, the Fairfax plantation near Mount Vernon.

It was hard for George Washington to forget his love for Sally Fairfax, since he often visited Belvoir. George's

A portrait of Lawrence Washington in 1738. *Mount Vernon Ladies' Association.*

half-brother Lawrence had married Colonel Fairfax's daughter, Anne. Also, Colonel Fairfax thought George was a person who one day could become a leader in Virginia. The older man took a fatherly interest in him. George's own father had died, so he chose as heroes—models for his own life—Lawrence and Colonel Fairfax. They were the two men who encouraged him and gave him a start in his career.

In 1752 Lawrence Washington died. By the terms of his will George eventually inherited Mount Vernon. Still in his early twenties, George's future as a wealthy gentleman farmer in Virginia seemed secure.

Washington was appointed county surveyor in 1749. The compass he used has been preserved. *Smithsonian Institution.*

But George, ambitious, wanted more than wealth alone. He had grander things in mind. Less than two years after Lawrence's death, he got his chance.

Great Britain and France long had been enemies. They were rivals for control of western lands in America. When French traders and soldiers began to build forts along the Ohio River, the British grew alarmed. Governor Dinwiddie of Virginia decided to send a messenger to the French, warning them to leave or British soldiers would drive them out. He needed someone young enough and strong enough to make the difficult trip through the wilderness. But he also needed a person of good judgment, manners, and charm who could deal with the French leaders. Governor Dinwiddie chose George Washington.

During a trip of eleven weeks covering nearly one thousand miles, George was shot at by Indians and once fell from his raft into an icy river. But he returned safely. The French, he now knew, would not leave peacefully. His report to Governor Dinwiddie was read throughout the American colonies and in England.

Next, in the spring of 1754, Washington was ordered to lead a small force of Virginia soldiers into the wilderness. He was to reach the place where Pittsburgh stands today, a spot that controlled the movement of traffic along the Ohio River.

He discovered that the French had already arrived and

built Fort Duquesne there. George still managed, however, to surprise a small party of French soldiers and win a victory over them. It was his first battle, and he liked it. "I have heard the bullets whistle," he later wrote to a friend, "and believe me, there is something charming in the sound."

In June 1755 the British sent a large force of regular soldiers, dressed in bright red uniforms, to capture Fort Duquesne. Their leader, General Edward Braddock, never before had fought a battle in America. He marched his soldiers through the woods in perfect order, as if they were on a parade ground in Europe. Wagons filled with supplies followed at the rear. Heavy cannons had to be hauled over the mountains.

George Washington, along as an aide to Braddock, warned him about the way the French and Indians fought, but Braddock would not listen. Slowly the British approached Fort Duquesne.

One day they were marching along a narrow road cut through the forest. A fife and drum played at the front of the long column of troops. Suddenly, the French and Indians attacked. Their gunfire seemed to come from behind every tree.

Braddock fell wounded. The red-coated British soldiers, jammed together on the road, made easy targets. Many died instantly. Indians, rushing from their hiding places, tomahawked the wounded. Then, thoroughly

Jacob Vannebrames et Robert Scobo tous
deux capitaines, nous seront remis en olaye
jusqua larrivee de nos Canadiens et francois
cy dessus mentionnés.

nous nous obligeons de notre coté a
donner lescorte pour Remener en Sureté les
deux officiers qui nous promettent nos
francois dans deux mois et demi pour
le plus tard

fait double Sur un des postes de
notre blocus cejour et an que dessus

James Mackay G. Washington

Coulon Villier

A surrender document in French, signed at Fort Necessity by Washington, the French commander, and a British captain. *Samuel Collection, Royal Museum of Ontario.*

frightened, the surviving British soldiers threw down their weapons and ran.

George Washington tried to stop them from running away. He had two horses shot out from under him. Bullets passed through his clothing. Almost miraculously, he was unhurt.

The British were badly defeated. For months afterward, Indians raided frontier posts and killed the settlers. Meanwhile, word of Washington's courage near Fort Duquesne spread through the American colonies. He was put in charge of defending Virginia against the French and Indians.

The war between France and England lasted until 1763, with the British finally winning a total, smashing victory.

During the war, in 1759, something important happened to George Washington. He married. His bride was a widow, Martha Dandridge Custis. She, like George, was about twenty-six when they married. Cheerful, good-natured, and good-looking, she had two children, a boy and a girl, from her first marriage.

She also happened to be one of the richest women in America. The new Mrs. Washington owned several hundred acres of fine farmland and hundreds of slaves.

The Washingtons, with plenty of money to spend, added to Mount Vernon by buying nearby farms. They entertained many visitors. They lived a pleasant life:

dancing, playing cards, visiting, fox hunting.

But the life of the gentleman farmer was far from easy. Washington worked hard. He had to look after the planting of wheat and tobacco and be sure that the farm animals had good care. Then he had to sell whatever was produced at Mount Vernon. There were letters to write to England, bills to be paid, clothing and shoes to be made for the workers. Washington also won election many times to the House of Burgesses, where he helped make the laws of Virginia.

He came to be known by the Masons, the Lees, the Burwells—some of Virginia's most influential families. He was an officer in his church. And he helped start a company to get more land to the west, land he hoped to sell for a large profit. By 1774, when he was forty-two, his life seemed peaceful and settled.

All that would soon change.

The winners of a war sometimes have more serious problems than the losers. After defeating France in 1763, the British found themselves the rulers of enormous territories, including Canada and India. To hire soldiers and public officials for service in such places is expensive. Meanwhile, the British had to protect the American colonists against the Indians. That cost money, too. They also had to pay back all they had borrowed to fight their global war against France.

Where would the money come from? The American

A portrait of Martha Dandridge Custis painted by John Wollaston a short time before she was widowed in 1757. *Washington/Custis/Lee Collection, Washington and Lee University, Lexington, Virginia.*

The piazza on the eastern side of Mount Vernon, with a view of the Potomac River, one of Washington's favorite places. *Paul Rocheleau, Rebus, Inc.*

colonies, said Great Britain, should at least be willing to help pay for their own defense. That was only fair.

But getting the colonists to agree to new taxes was not easy. Americans had gotten used to ruling themselves. They did not like the idea of Parliament—the lawmakers in faraway England—telling them what to do and how much tax to pay.

In Virginia, George Washington was one of those who did not like being bossed by the British. He said little in public, but he talked to his powerful friends and wrote letters to them. In one letter he wrote: "I think the Parliament of Great Britain hath no more right to put their hands into my pocket, without my consent, than I have to put my hands in yours for money."

Great Britain tried harder and harder to force America to obey. Instead, the Americans only grew more angry. Virginia elected George Washington and six other men to the First Continental Congress, held at Philadelphia. There, leaders from the colonies talked about what they should do next.

The other leaders liked Washington. They liked the way he looked: tall, strong, completely in control of his body. And with all the confusion and talk in Philadelphia, they liked his calm, quiet, good sense. He did most of his talking in small groups or at the dinner table. As in Virginia, people trusted Washington. They thought he was honest, fair, and steady.

In the next few months, excitement grew. British troops clashed with American "Minutemen" in Massachusetts at Lexington and Concord. By May 1775, when the Second Continental Congress met, the British had decided to send a large army to crush the colonists.

Among the leaders of the Second Continental Congress, George Washington had the most experience as

General Washington's portable case in which he carried his field equipment, including tin plates and knives. *Charles Phillips, National Museum of American History.*

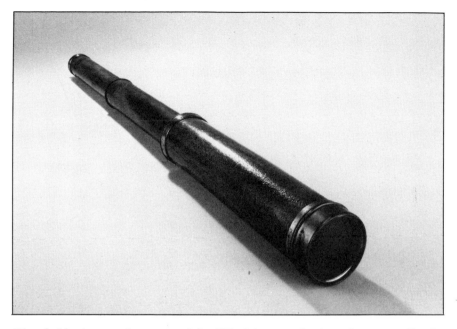

The field glass and case used by Washington during the war. *Charles Phillips, Lewis Collection, National Museum of American History.*

a soldier: seven years of fighting on the frontier. He was the person chosen to make plans for a Continental army, just in case the colonies had to defend themselves. When the time actually came to choose a commander for the army, Washington was the only choice. Everyone regarded him as the right man for the job—calm under fire, dependable, a man of high character—a general who could be trusted. Besides, he was an example for those people in the colonies still undecided about the war. If a man of such wealth and good judgment favored the American cause, maybe it made sense.

Washington got every vote for the post of army commander. He had not asked for the job, but he thought it was his duty to take it. With quiet dignity, he agreed.

On July 3, 1775, Washington took charge of the army, then facing the British outside Boston. He could not know that what lay ahead were years of bloody fighting, cold, hunger, and bitter disappointment. And if he failed, his almost-certain fate would be death by hanging—as an outlaw and traitor to the king of England.

The army Washington took over included at first no more than fifteen thousand men—largely untrained and with no patience for military discipline. Everything the soldiers needed was in short supply: guns, ammunition, food, clothing, tents, blankets. Most of the men had enlisted for only one year. When it was time to do planting or harvesting on their farms, many of them simply walked away from camp. Congress, meanwhile, failed to raise enough money to pay the officers and men of the army. To support their families, many of them were forced to go home.

In the beginning the Americans won a few victories. General Ethan Allen captured Fort Ticonderoga and opened the way for a possible invasion of Canada. Washington himself freed Boston from British control.

But soon it became clear to Washington that the war would be long and hard. After a year of struggle the Americans stopped fighting for their rights as English-

General Washington's wartime tent. *Charles Phillips, National Museum of American History.*

men. They decided to fight for freedom—for a country all their own. They signed the Declaration of Independence.

It was one thing, however, to declare independence, another thing to win it. Washington knew that the British had more soldiers, more ships, more money. But he hoped that, if the fighting went on, the British would tire of the war. They would agree to America's freedom and go home.

Battle followed battle. But neither side could knock out the other. Still, by the end of 1777 Washington thought that his plan was beginning to work. The British had failed to destroy his army. Meanwhile, at Saratoga, New York, on October 17, 1777, an entire British force under General Burgoyne—an army numbering seventeen thousand men—had surrendered.

America's victory at Saratoga was vital. It convinced the French that perhaps, with help, the ragged, untrained Americans could defeat mighty Great Britain. If so, then France might one day win back her lost empire in the New World. The French already were giving some help secretly, but after Saratoga they decided to show themselves openly as America's friends. They signed a treaty of alliance—a friendship agreement. In it they promised to help America win freedom from Great Britain.

News of the alliance with France brought cheer to Washington's troops, then in winter quarters near Philadelphia, at Valley Forge. Many of the soldiers at Valley Forge had no shoes. Their feet left traces of blood in the snow where they walked. Their uniforms were nothing but rags. Still they trusted General Washington. They fought on.

Washington reviewing his troops at Valley Forge. *Valley Forge Historical Society.*

By now Washington was a familiar figure to his men. They had seen his bravery in battle. With cannon shots whizzing past his ears and landing by his feet, he remained completely calm, peering through his spy glass. Sometimes he would stroll without concern in open sight of the enemy. He charged, alone, into the heart of a battle.

Yet Washington was no fool. He was more like a fox, using surprise attacks, slyly moving his troops to unexpected places, catching the enemy off balance. Once he moved his entire army by night, fooling the British by leaving the campfires burning. He was one of history's finest generals.

In camp, away from battle, he relaxed. He would pick up a ball and play catch with his aides. Or he would compete with them at throwing weights. With his great strength he could throw farther than any of them. He towered tall above everyone in camp, and they held him in awe.

The war continued, with first one side, then the other, seeming to win. Finally, General Cornwallis, the British commander, made a serious mistake. He allowed himself to be penned in against the sea at Yorktown, Virginia, expecting that his troops would be taken off by ships. Washington saw his chance and pounced like a tiger. He marched from New Jersey to face Cornwallis on land, while the French Admiral De Grasse cut off any British escape by sea. On October 17, 1781, under heavy artillery bombardment, Cornwallis surrendered.

After Washington's great victory at Yorktown, the remaining British forces soon gave up. A treaty of peace was signed in Paris in September 1783, ending the war. Great Britain agreed to give independence to the Americans.

At Fraunces' Tavern in New York City, Washington said farewell to the officers of his army, men he had fought beside through years of bitter combat. Many of them wept. Washington himself, usually stern and con-

A French view of the Battle of Yorktown. *Anne S. K. Brown Military Collection, Brown University.*

trolled in public, could not bring himself to speak. He simply embraced each of his comrades in silence. By Christmas Eve, 1783, he was home at Mount Vernon with Martha.

George Washington was barely past the age of fifty when the war ended. Yet he felt old and tired. He and Martha had no children of their own, and both of Martha's children by her first marriage had died. Her son, Jack, had died of disease at the Battle of Yorktown. The Washingtons adopted Jack's children and brought them to live at Mount Vernon.

As time passed, George became more and more worried about the new American nation. He thought the

A painting by Alonzo Chappel of General Washington's farewell to his officers December 4, 1783. *Chicago Historical Society.*

government was too weak. There was no army. Britain, France, and Spain openly insulted the Americans. The states argued with one another. But, tired, George Washington did not again want to leave the peace and quiet of his life as a gentleman farmer.

In 1786, unhappy farmers in western Massachusetts led by Daniel Shays marched across the state, armed with muskets and pitchforks. Their "rebellion" was put down. But Washington decided that he had to do something. Otherwise, wealthy people would have an excuse for demanding a king. They would say that a very strong government was needed, one that told people what to do. Mobs would run wild, breaking the law. Washington did not want mobs to rule. But neither did he want a king. After all, Americans had just fought a revolution to get rid of one king. Why have another?

On May 13, 1787, Washington arrived for a meeting in Philadelphia. The meeting, which lasted through the summer, came to be known as the Constitutional Convention. The purpose of the Convention was to write a better set of rules for governing the people of America. George met many of his old friends: Benjamin Franklin, James Madison, Alexander Hamilton, John Adams.

They elected Washington president of the Convention. Who else could have stayed calm and fair while so many talented, educated men argued excitedly about what the American government should be like? Day after

The president's chair that Washington occupied at the Constitutional Convention. At the close of the convention, as delegates were signing the Constitution, Benjamin Franklin commented that in the course of the convention he had often wondered whether the sun carved on the back of the chair was rising or setting. "Now, at length," he said, "I have the happiness to know that it is a rising and not a setting sun." *George Fistrovich, National Park Service.*

day, Washington listened patiently. He soothed ruffled tempers and called on speakers in turn so they would not shout at each other.

At last the work of the Convention ended. What had come out of that summer in Philadelphia was the Constitution of the United States of America. Few men who worked on the Constitution liked every part of it. Some were deeply disappointed. But as Washington said, it was the best that could be done at the time. Now, more than two centuries later, we know that it is one of the great documents in the history of human freedom.

In 1788 the time came to choose a president for the new government. Everyone agreed it should be George Washington. By then he was in his mid fifties and his brown hair was graying. But he still walked and rode with grace. Well over six feet tall, powerfully built, he stood erect and with great dignity. He had, said one foreign visitor, "the soul, look, and figure of a hero."

On April 30, 1789, Washington became the first president of the United States under the new Constitution. He took no fancy title, such as *His Highness* or *His Mightiness,* as some people suggested, just the simple *Mr. President.*

The city that one day would bear his name was still being built. So Washington lived at first in a small house on Cherry Street in New York City, then the nation's capital. He rode out on his horse for two hours in the morning, went to church on Sunday, and gave regular parties—something he thought a head of government should do. Occasionally he took trips to New England or the South to see how the country was doing.

Washington liked to get along with people. He could disagree with someone and still be that person's friend. He believed that people came to a problem with differing

A painting of George Washington, en route to his inauguration in New York, being greeted by the citizens of Trenton, New Jersey. *John and Lillian Harvey, Trenton, New Jersey.*

backgrounds, so they were bound to disagree. Still, he thought that honorable men would place the public good over their own personal wishes. If they did, then good will would win out. In his own life he had learned to check his temper and use his energy for good. The result had been much like a powerful wild stallion under perfect control.

Other men, however, did not have George Washington's strength—or his common sense. For the eight years of his presidency he watched with anguish as his beloved countrymen bickered and fought with each other. It all started in his own cabinet. The clever, ambitious Alexander Hamilton, secretary of the Treasury, stood squarely against Thomas Jefferson, secretary of state and one of the best-educated leaders in America's history.

Hamilton believed in a very strong central government controlled by a few men of great wealth and property. He favored big business and commerce and hoped that the United States and Great Britain would be close friends.

Jefferson believed in as little government as possible. He thought that big cities and industry would ruin the nation. Only a nation of farmers, each looking after his own plot of land, would bring the happiness that Jefferson thought was best. In foreign affairs, Jefferson favored friendship with Britain's deadly enemy, France.

Both Hamilton and Jefferson had followers. Soon those

followers banded together into political parties, like today's Republicans and Democrats. Washington hated
the idea of parties. He thought that all Americans should
work together for the good of the country, regardless of
party labels.

Vainly he tried to stop Hamilton and Jefferson from
ripping the country in two. Like a father, he talked with
both men. He wrote letter after letter to them, pleading
that each should give in a little.

An engraving of Washington's inauguration on the balcony of Federal
Hall in New York City, from a drawing by Peter Lacour. *I. N. Phelps
Stokes Collection, New York Public Library.*

Oil portraits by Charles Willson Peale of Thomas Jefferson (*left*) and Alexander Hamilton (*right*). *Independence National Historical Park Collection.*

Washington was not as clever as Hamilton. He was not as well educated or cultured as Jefferson. But he had better judgment than either. He was steadier. He had better control of himself. He had a clearer understanding of what America needed at the time. And, unlike Hamilton and Jefferson, he didn't have to have his way on everything. He could give in sometimes.

Washington's first four years as president drained him of energy. He was tired. He wanted to return to Mount

Washington with Martha and her grandchildren in 1796, in an oil-on-canvas portrait by Edward Savage. George Washington Parke Custis stands at left; Eleanor Parke Custis stands beside her grandmother. A servant, William Lee, stands at the right. *Andrew W. Mellon Collection, National Gallery of Art, Washington, D.C.*

Vernon. He craved his quiet life as a farmer. But he knew that, with all the quarreling between the followers of Jefferson and Hamilton, the country still needed him. In 1792 he agreed, unwillingly, to stay on for another four-year term. It was his duty. Again he was elected without opposition.

During Washington's second term the nation grew stronger. New states were added. When General "Mad Anthony" Wayne defeated the Indians in the Battle of Fallen Timbers, the Ohio River Valley was made safe for settlers. Because of Hamilton's work as secretary of the Treasury, people in the United States and in other countries trusted the dollar. They knew that the American government paid its debts.

Meanwhile, Washington kept the nation out of war. He refused to side with either England or France in their great conflict. All America needed, said Washington, was time—several years of peace. After that, the country would be so rich, and would have so many people, that it could defend itself. Until then, Washington sometimes had to sign treaties that looked like bad bargains. They gave the United States less than most Americans wanted. But the treaties were the best that the new government could get. And, just as Washington hoped, they kept the peace and bought the nation time to grow strong.

Finally, in the summer of 1796, Washington announced that he would not serve a third term. In March 1797, John Adams of Massachusetts became president. George and Martha Washington returned to Mount Vernon.

Out of office, the heavy burden removed from his shoulders, Washington still found much to do. Mount

A view of Mount Vernon, painted in oils about 1790. *National Gallery of Art, Washington. Gift of Edgar William and Bernice Chrysler Garbisch.*

Vernon needed repairs, and only he could direct the work. Letters had to be written. Famous painters wanted him to pose for pictures. A steady stream of visitors came to see him, including favorite old friends like the French general Lafayette. Once, in 1798, it seemed that America would have to go to war, and President Adams asked Washington to command the army. But the problem was solved peacefully.

Growing older, Washington no longer hunted foxes or danced. But he still enjoyed riding on horseback around the spacious fields of Mount Vernon.

Washington's study at Mount Vernon, a room in which he worked for several hours each day and all day Sunday. He purchased the secretary desk at right near the end of his presidency. In the corner is a fan chair; when the foot pedal was pressed, the fan above the chair moved back and forth. The letterpress in the foreground was a primitive copying device. *Mount Vernon Ladies' Association.*

One cold, snowy day, though, he rode through the fields for several hours. He returned home wet and chilled to the bone. The next day his throat was sore, and he had trouble breathing. No medicine seemed to help. His doctors tried the standard remedies of the time: molasses and butter, rum, vinegar. Finally they drew blood from his body with leeches. Nothing worked. Washington grew steadily weaker.

On December 14, 1799, just two days after his illness began, George Washington died. He was nearly sixty-eight years old.

Like everything else in his life, Washington had faced death with quiet courage. He had looked over his will, making sure, for example, that after his death all of his slaves would be given their freedom.

Americans knew they had lost a great leader. So did the rest of the world. The French remembered him as a friend. The British, meeting Washington first as an enemy, had come to admire him as a brave general and a gentleman. In time, his fame grew even greater. Countless places were named after him—streets, towns, counties, states, rivers, schools—even the city that became the nation's capital. Today, in the distant People's Republic of China, he is one of the few people in American history known to the Chinese—the leader who led Americans in a revolution to free themselves from foreign rule.

The bed in which Washington died. *Mount Vernon Ladies' Association.*

These oil-on-canvas portraits of George and Martha Washington, by John Trumbull, hung in their bedroom at Mount Vernon. *Lewis Collection, National Museum of American History.*

Over the years many myths grew up around the life of Washington, such as the story of his chopping down the cherry tree or helping Betsy Ross make the first American flag. But the truth is even more to Washington's credit than the myths. Historians who study his life come away from their work with new respect for him. They praise his fierce willpower in staying with a task, such as the Revolution, until it was finished. They speak of his wisdom as a ruler. Unlike some later presidents, Washington refused ever to do anything he knew was wrong. Most of all, his life stands as an example of a leader who, regardless of the cost to himself, did his duty.

As a young man growing up in the glamorous society of Virginia, Washington was unsure of himself and feared failure. Eventually he became so strong in character that he was the one man America could not do without. Because of the ever-growing mastery that George Washington won over himself, the story of his life deserves to be studied by each new generation of American young people.

From such a study they can learn the lesson of personal growth through hard work. From his life, too, they can learn that sometimes in overcoming difficulties the most important qualities are good sense, good character, and staying power.

FOR FURTHER READING

Many books have been written about Washington. By far the most complete is Douglas Southall Freeman's massive six volume work, *George Washington* (1948–54), with a seventh volume written by his associates. James T. Flexner also has prepared a multivolumed biography, followed by his brilliant study *George Washington: The Indispensable Man* (1975). For insights into Washington's personality, two especially valuable sources are Marcus Cunliffe, *George Washington: Man and Monument* (1982) and Charles C. Wall, *George Washington* (1982).

INDEX